Elegy
for a
Star Girl

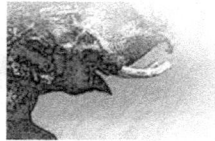

Elegy for a Star Girl

by
Christopher Grillo

This book is dedicated to my mother, Dolores.

Thank you for insisting on all that exists beyond the life I thought I knew, for encouraging me to reach for it, and showing me the best way to do so: with feet firmly planted on the ground.

Without you, there are no worlds (or even words) to fill this great void.

Ti amo.

Contents

I. The Other World

ANECDOTE: FOR THE UNINTENDED JOURNEY......................... 11

LIFTOFF 12

HOT AIR...13

PROOF 17

NIGHT-TIME 19

THE EFFECT OF SPACEFLIGHT ON THE HUMAN BODY..........21

STAR CITY I 23

STAR CITY II... 24

ANECDOTE: FOR TRYING TO REDISCOVER SOMETHING YOU
WEREN'T LOOKING FOR THE FIRST TIME 25

ENTROPY... 27

II. The Here and Now

HUMILITY 31

RULES OF LONG DURATION SPACE TRAVEL........................ 32

MY SILENT DINNER COMPANION 34

CREATION 36

THE BEQUEATHED 37

AURORA BOREALIS..38

ELEGY FOR A STAR GIRL 39

III. Transcendence

THINGS I MISS OF HOME.. 43

PERCEPTION AND REALITY 45

BLINDED 47

HOME RUN 49

GRAVITATIONAL LENSING 51
QUANTUM 52
PETALS.. 53
SYMMETRY... 56
THE DEATH OF STAR 58

I.
The Other World

Anecdote: For the Unintended Journey

You are driving down a road you do not recognize. You turned down this road, so there was a point in the not so distant past when you knew exactly where you were going. There are gas stations and phone poles and street lamps and an illusion of familiarity, but you are realizing that you are lost. This anxiety washes over you slowly, but you convince yourself that you will eventually spot a familiar landmark, and so you press on. You see nothing, but you have long since stopped looking. If you were going to turn around it should have been miles ago. The place from whence you came now feels like another world, a bleaker world, where something hanging in the air dulled the color of any splendid thing, so that no one knew to regard it as splendid.

Liftoff

What will it be like?
The coldest day
of your life, until
it's the warmest

you remember
in years. The sun
will shine, the water
off the harbor lap

against rocks. You
will hear all of this,
and then you will hear
ignition, feel a tremor,

and all at once
a quaking. Then
you will only hear
regret,

and God's voice,
three *g's* worth
of exasperation,

and you will be sure
that man was never
meant for this.

Hot Air

I dreamt to launch from Cape Canaveral
so imagine ten hours of lament, across
ocean and the tundra to Balkonur,
what that does to a man.

I have lost myself in the rearview thinking
of that earth bound flight, laughing as
blue sphere shrinks in perfect proportion,
the sluggish deflating of the only thing
that was ever in sight, leaking its grandeur

until it is just one of a hundred, thousand,
million latex balloons let loose from small
hands to rest arbitrarily against a deep, black
drop ceiling, the very fabric of space and time.

Of course, there are no rearview mirrors
on the ship, but someone doodled across
the cabin monitor: objects are closer
than they appear. Nothing could be farther
from the truth.

Mantras (I.) for the Destination

You know those people you hate,
the ones who stop foot traffic in
the middle of Grand Central to
pose for pictures faux biting
kiosk bagels? Be like them.

Stop trying to look like you've
been here before. Apparent
captivation is endearing.

There is such a thing as coming on
too strong.

The Opportunist

I am a lonesome traveler, but I was alone
so long before I ever was a traveler.

What inspires someone to leave
everything they've ever known

is the recognition that all of it,
each existing body, its comprised matter,

is doomed, sentenced by universal
law to ruin. The earth is large

to the static man who does not know
this, and so he may fool himself

into thinking he has escaped,
but if he lives long enough

he will be forced to reckon with the
absence of whatever he has run from,

and then it will find him.
Off orbit, within the confines

of atmosphere, nothing happens
that doesn't happen everywhere else,

but to be here at dawn is definitively
novice. I call it dawn only because

to call it what it is when particles bend

light this drastically would lose you.
In all directions, everything

is unaltered or altered so much
its ripeness is overwhelming.

Proof

The universe contains everything.
Amidst everything, there is a set of elements H,
human kind, and within this set, there's me,
lowercase x, before you. Little x exists
in other subsets of set H (sets of elements
stubborn, angry, benevolent, trying desperately
to show this to the world, but failing).

Then there is y, you before me, which exists
in this same set H, one grain of the cosmos
washed over and refined by inertia and nebulae
sediment, slow dancing throughout your own
respective subsets.

Let us assume that L is a function, a place
where the thing that changed me the moment
I met you filled every inch of space with the density
of a neutron star so that there was no room
for doubt or the kind of tangential thought
that shifts the affections of young, brash men.

We entered it together, a dusty bar on the north
end of town where I could barely hear you speak
over beer league softball teams losing audible
reasonability after shots of Jameson.

 If X is a set, a new union of elements contained
 in the subsets of H I called home,
then for every element x in X
there is exactly one and only one element y

such that the ordered pair (x, y), me and you,
is contained in the subset definition, the function L.

Night-time

Each sol ends colder than the last. The sky
at dusk is blood shot, the suns vicinity

a powder blue iris, cataract covered.
This is the problem with small elastic

scattering probability: all color dingy.
In this way, sunset's scheme disproves

the truth I've known of rush hour on earth.
It is the definition of other worldly.

The first time I saw, I cried,
not over beauty, or immense separate place,
but because this is all it took.

Mantras (II.) for the Return...

You are equipped for this. You've
been training your whole life.
Think life after pizza.

This will be worse. It tasted
better.

Missing is a much stronger
emotion than loving.

Frozen Yogurt will never be ice
cream.

The Effect of Spaceflight on the Human Body

We do not orbit but free float,
letting go of what binds *us* to ourselves.

We touch worlds where language fails
and form loses permanence,

where we hike or eat Thai food despite
our former assertions that tamarind powder

and palm sugar mask incidental
flavor and that hiking, which is neither

a relaxed or strenuous physical state,
is confusing. For thousands of hours,

we drift. We span light years, but *how long*,
and *how far*, are less pressing questions

than *why*. We know the answer. It is as obvious
to us as breath, and fills us the same way,

but it is measurable only in simile: *we fought
like braves, we made love like strangers,*

and so it demands we reimagine distance and time
with wild, limitless depth. We sink willingly

and too fast. We are pressed until we break
and customize like warm forged steel that seeps

through its contour and is left to cool as polytopes
when black smiths are busy kissing.

We pray we will be left blunted, not sleek,
and that this will slow us when we fall,

because we will fall, or gravitate back towards,
or reenter, which are all the same thing,

and only mistaken to be dissimilar
by cataloguers who lie, and the drag

coefficient, which is a lie. Let there be no mistake.
No matter how fast, we will plummet.

No matter how hot, we will burn.
No matter how hard, we will crash,

and the finite world we once swore could never
be swallowed whole, will leave us wanting.

Star City I.

A cosmonaut wakes smiling
not because he is supremely happy
but because for a moment,
with his consciousness
still anchored by sleep, he is met
again with space euphoria, falling
in elliptical orbit at 17,000 mph.
He understands depth perception
well, but forgets for a moment,
or perhaps ignores, the masquerade.
His moon boots dance across
the surface of the ocean
below him, his *chasse*
responsible for the streaking
of cumulous clouds that marbleize
the world's veneer. Ground control
works to prepare for reentry
and he ignores, risking the rate
of air tank expenditure
and his suit's will to maintain
stable pressurization. He swims
in his sheets, a baby in utero,
his contention unparalleled,
unencumbered by all he has seen,
reacted to, or been catalyst for.

Star City II.

A cosmonaut wrestling a Moskvich gear stick,
down, over, and up: reverse. It is a finicky
machine, but gets the job done, and easy
to troubleshoot with a ball point hammer
to the spark plugs.

There is a jolt, or a word like jolt [or lurch]
for when things which were still are suddenly
moving, but there is no accelerative climb,
merely a point where motion began —
the entry interface.

He does not bother to check rear view mirrors,
trusts the starkness of star city in winter,
flakes of stucco rolling across the parking lot
like tumbleweed. The sun is high, bouncing
off the iced over chrome of the rear bumper
and bending past his peripheries like drag spark
off the heat shield.

Now with his wits about him, the cosmonaut
can slow burn. He pumps pre-antilock brakes
with little finesse. Each time there is whiplash
on the frame and the body strapped to it,
necessary to mark division in meters per second
until he is at a final and disappointing rest.

Anecdote: For Trying to Rediscover Something You Weren't Looking for the First Time

We drove home from summer parties beer glazed with hormones flared so hot you could see them, red like electric stove coils. The first time she took me to her spot (that's what she called it) I thought for sure we would get caught. It wasn't anywhere remote like I'd expected, but right on the side of the road. She asked me to trust her, that if I pulled about 20 steps from the corner, about 8 steps out into the street, we'd be blind from any vantage. Years later, I bumped into her at a bar. We were a bit older, a bit more skeptical of love, and more cavalier with sex. We left together, glazed again but in something stronger and more expensive. She asked where we should go and I told her I knew just the place, but that it was a surprise. I remembered the street names I used to drive past to get there (it's funny what's living on the surface of the subconscious) but not exactly where I was going and figured once I got close, the way would come back to me and muscle memory would guide my hands through the turns. She played along, covered her eyes and giggled in the passenger seat, giddy because she knew exactly what I was up to. It started to feel like too long a drive, so I turned up the radio to distract her and mask the horny frustration that sounded each time I passed a place that looked like it might be but wasn't. When I finally pulled over I knew I wasn't there, but what was the difference really? I turned to her, asked if she was ready for the big reveal. It must have just happened on the last frantic sweep through those old roads. At first I thought she was still playing along, her eyes still closed, slouched low in her chair. But then I switched off the radio, heard the sounds of sleeping breath, and then a sudden drunk guttural snore, and I knew we'd never be there again.

Entropy

Perhaps it is not the star girl that I miss,
but rather our domain: the space
we entered that made us what we were.

I am in search of a newness,
something that could step in
and continue to refine me.

Nothing that is earthbound
can play the part as she did,

and because the butterfly dies
a butterfly, and no thing
in this universe reverts

to its former self,
I travel with a prayer
that an element exists

amidst the void capable
of filling me to the point
that I bloom and explode

in a spectacle so awe inspiring
that it can only be described
as chaos.

II.
The Here and
the Now

Mantras (III.) for the Present

When implored to use the word to describe when you are going to do something, remember that "now" is a state and not an increment of time.

In the grand scheme of the cosmos, humans are rare. Be good to folks.

In the grand scheme of the cosmos, humans are rare, and in no way central to its purpose.

When you give names to stuff, you ignore complexity.

Words are a construction of man, and thus reality's very distant cousin.

Somewhere in the world, an artist is losing his mind trying to describe the very specific beauty of a sunset.

Humility

The best thing about the star girl, (the best
quality I have known in any person,

but she is emblematic of its scarcity)
was her recognition of her own absolute

meaninglessness (which coursed through
her veins, and ran parallel to white blood cells).

She knew nothing of astrological units,
the average radius of the Earth's orbit,

$1.4960 * 10^{11}$ meters. Despite this the star
girl self-effaced as though it were her anatomy.

How could any modest person exist
who does not know that the distance light

travels through a frictionless vacuum,
unencumbered for one full year,

is equivalent to nearly 10 million blind
human revolutions around the sun?

Still the star girl smiled at things threatening
to ruin her days, (angry retailers, trainee waitresses,

traffic jams) and vaguely regarded
her time, which she felt was unpretentious

because one day the whole lot of it would be but a blip.

Rules of Long Duration Space Travel

This is no country
for a young man, no country
at all, just landscape.

We are untethered.
You have time left for regrets:
take it, all of it.

There are specs of life
worth reminiscence: betray
them not. Look again.

Again and again
the night sky called you nearer:
chase something closer.

She moves to spite you.
The last word ends, ellipses,
and you're on page 1.

Don't mistake inquiry
for pining, or worse yet, love
which is anguish,

rocket propulsion
against the grain of atmosphere.
You will just burn up.

Long before you reach
one light, the void will have stretched.

Years after you die

the moon will only
have moved inches, the oldest
stars will still hold strong.

My Silent Dinner Companion

There is so much here that I do not
have words for. I believe this now
to be a blessing. In the sterility
of my sleeping quarters my mind
moves in anecdotes. This is vital.

A cave dwelling man, though he
does not denote himself as such,
eats dinner with a woman
with whom he shares his cave,
but whom he does not have words
for like wife, partner, lover, etc.

He glances at her adoringly,
and she knows that it is either
because he actually admires her,
or because he wants her to cut
him another steak from the caribou
hide that she has perfectly undercooked

over the fire at the center of their cave.
She would be wrong to think the latter.
He knows she could have chosen
any other place on earth and it would
have been the same as this.

He appreciates that, and even though
she cannot be sure of what lies behind
his adoring look, she rises, three leg
walks across the cave floor and hacks
at the fleshy region of inner thigh

on the animal, not because
he has told her he likes this part,
but because she has observed
how seriously he takes the challenge

of chewing it completely,
and this, to her, is striking.

Creation

There is so much science does not know
like why the God particle should have
collapsed the cosmos and didn't.

It is my contention that things do not
collapse other things, but that cornerstones
recede and bolsters rot, and covered

in the star dust that would make up man,
He saw that man would give Him a name,
fear and worship him, and He was pleased,

but then He saw that man would kill,
again and again, mostly in the name
of God, gnawing at the stuff

of life like termites until rafters failed
and the roof caved. Still, He saw
there could be a little light, little bits

like you that could stop languishing souls
in their tracks, turn takers and sayers
into good men, and so the Higgs

threaded His needle and joined matter
with a welt seam letting the likes
of you shine so we could all see Saturn's
rings first hand.

The Bequeathed

The impressionists gave us a lens, a way
to see a world that we had lost sight of.
We did not look through it, out at all
we'd inherited, but upon it. We built
cities, knocked them down, and made
them taller, and when the impressionists
died we hung their paintings on our white
walls, argued over the length of brushstrokes
and said "look what man has made!"

We put starry night on coffee mugs
and t shirts, where it lost it purposeful
dimensions, the steeple that rises above
the village and the cypress that weaves
through the sky and past the morning
star like scaffolding for the dead to climb
past to the edge of the canvas, just one
of innumerable and arbitrary horizons.

Aurora Borealis

Solar winds crack like a whip,
leave scars on this world's hide,
but no tissue builds to callous
the shell; it is simply chipped
away chunk by chunk.

Imagine what man would be
if every bump, bruise, scrape,
scratch, slice, and lash left him
less, weakened skin instead
of leathering?

It is amazing to me how much
we have taken for granted
earth's magnetism. So much
so, Yukon country hosts

backpacking tourists
so the aurora can be checked
off a grand list of landmarks.
I have never been. I wonder

if there is plaque on a fir
in British Columbia that calls
the northern lights what they are:
shrapnel. The collateral damages
of a war waged by the life
giving sun.

Elegy for a Star Girl

I.

Remember the bone roads, the closest to the city
where we could see stars and we chose instead
to smoke out your Nissan, cloud the sunroof
with smog, little better than oilmen
in our singular search for a strong buzz,
my singular search for your tongue, just damp
and drying quickly from the weed but not
disappointing, never disappointing.

We are too old not to have been driving
when the Hale Bop comet screamed over head.
We were too young to notice, too damn high
to separate mine from yours, just the body
in pieces slowly braiding together.
We will never be there again.

II.

There is little difference between what is known
and what is assumed to be known. Of course
that is only true if what is assumed is done
with adequate fervor. When this happens,
what is imagined to be true is as fundamental
as the molecular properties of water, H_2O,
the bedrock of life, which is what man drinks,
and how he cleans himself of sin.
I think this is what faith is.

You would have shamed me from this journey,

just as you would have shamed the mulling over
of these notions. You would not have done so
overtly, but in the breath of your own simplicity,
and the thing in you that believed singing hymns
to perennials at February's bitter end inspired
fuller blooms, though you'd never thought
to measure against a control set of globeflower.

III.

I have seen more here than most: sixteen
sunsets daily, and each one begs; brail over
the earth's surface, but the high peak at Everest
falls miles short of atmosphere, is nothing
to Olympus Mons, which is 400 days away
and the very next planet. Still I cannot assume
to know anything more than this: beyond the farthest
point in the known universe, the starting line ends.
Somewhere beyond that, there are answers to questions
rendered unimportant to men who know what it is
to be cut down with just one look.

Mulling over life is not living, which is why you
believed it just when the great poets died alone,
too busy pontificating on love to set aside time
for actual loving.

III.
Transcendence

Mantras (IV.) for Living and Dying and Living Again

The universe is not wasteful.
That's what humans are for.

Remember, the uncertainty principle. Your probabilities are limited by all your earthly impediments.

The body is man's only true hindrance.

Things I Miss of Home

The solace of cigarettes on lunch breaks
when I should be eating a sandwich.

Talking with the beggar outside
the deli on lunch breaks, sharing
a cigarette. I bought him orangeade
each day for a year so he could chase
his brown bag, which I hope was vodka.

Vodka. But mostly bourbon and red
wine. Not any vintage, but the jug juice
my father kept under the kitchen sink,
because there is nothing that warms
quite like it.

Anything the old man cooked me,
but especially hotdogs and eggs,
a real cowboy's dinner, though
I have missed this for longer
than I have eaten from vacuum seals.

The touch of a woman. Not just
any woman, but certainly any touch.

Gravity and my other earthly burdens,
for I am not yet displaced from the sight
of my former world; it still pleads at the edge
of my current horizon, a mother mouthing
"I love you" through the passenger side window
to her first born son, clumsily straining
to balance the weight of first day school supplies.

Perhaps that boy will about face and realize
what it is to be limitless.

Perception and Reality

Transmittal from early man
to Mars Col. Cruiser 3,
cabin number 4637,
through the very fabric
of space to a sleep starved
traveler with no sense of time

because he's moving through it
watching it all unfold:

We did not mistake the earth
for flat because we could not
see its curvature, but because
we were just not ready.

The universe's only truth
is fear: fear of what might
happen, fear of going without.

Light is a map fit to scale.
It charts what is there,
and makes it real.
But what about the paper
towns? What about
the cartographer's slip,

the things he misrepresents
because he's scared shitless
about his small place
in the world? I realize

now that everything I am,
I am because it serves
my own existence. I see
food when I am hungry.
I see water when I thirst.

I reckon with air
when I need to breathe
deeply. I fear the flame
not because it is orange,
or blue, or even white,

but because color is alarm,
and your face emblematic
of everything I could not
do without.

Blinded

The seeing lament
sun glare on television
screens. If we could feel

the weight of subway
filth on skin, compounded
and coated and sealed,

we'd know how truly
vulgar it is to be cased
so completely

in something foreign
to think it anything else
would be comforting.

This is what it is
to kiss her; each salient
molecule can be traced

by my tongues keen point.
I can taste glands and earl grey
that lingers despite

the sterility
of aspartame in Trident.
If I had one wish,

I'd be less present.
Palate numbed by her lip gloss;
I'd call it reverence.

I'd know it was love
that turned my stomach, or God.
I'd sing myself a wretch saved

for not seeing, hear
the busker's song and think it
worth every penny.

Home Run

A child has questions of color and shape
and the reasons why the physical world is,

curiosities too fundamental to satisfy
in a phrase and so they are shrugged

off with a single conjunction. The wanderings
of his mind are borne at night. He cocoons

in his New York Yankees comforter,
but he is unable to make out the pinstriped

pattern, or the shape of other shiny things
littered across this world that hold his thoughts

on orbit in the day time. Still, he is more certain
now of the *more* people say there *is* than in the seeing

hours. Soon his brain will have overdone it,
worn from the trillions

of snap shots it had strung together that afternoon
presenting a four seam fastball's trajectory.

And from pulling the levers and cranking
the cranks that signal the swing of the bat,

long before it reached the plane where he
would have thought it the right time to do so.

And from suppressing a smile as he rounded

the bases, head down, trying to act like he'd been

there before. In its weary state, the boy's mind
has deprioritized that kind of sad practicality,

the safe guarding of all the things he desperately
longs to scream out to the world, or declare to it,

or ask of it. This is why the boy dreams
of when he is grown and of straddling

the line between what he will do
and what he is capable of doing.

Gravitational Lensing

To observe the star girl was to understand
her many selves arranged as the compass rose,

each point staring at its antithesis. The revulsion
was powerful, and so self-loathing, the magnetism

of her aura, provided her soul's needle the truest
direction to follow. This was not how she existed

in the world, but how I knew her and that love
is tangible, massive, and dense: a body positioned

between two people that curves light and distorts
what is: the empty snifter presenting a brave new

world and the drunkard is audacious in never
assuming to know better.

Quantum

I feel closer to you here; I knew this to be true
long before I left. Do you remember church
as a child, heaven's promise reserved
for believers, all sin forgiven?

On earth, we are all dying from consumption,
swallowed by the roles we play, and choking
on their unwelcome aftertaste.

Marriage, family, career, community, nationality,
humanity. These are the nesting dolls
holding captive what we really are, conscious

stardust. I can feel you here, moving more gracefully,
or perhaps not moving, but just here, like a mist
that fills a room, free of everything that limited

you, free of physics, because you paid
ransom with your corpse. This is the luxury
afforded the sick, detachment from body,

strengthening of soul, the chance to look
into the eyes of the cosmos and see
the endlessness of probability.

Petals

Of the probable, the finite,
the familiar causality (actions
and reactions which feel
much like actions when
man is self-important),

there is one temporal coordinate
that leads me here. I am sure
it starts with a beach,
a sunset, a spontaneous
young couple with no sand
chairs or blanket to sit on.

2 solo cups,
(red),
a whole bottle of wine
split between them,
(red also).

A drum line: owners of all things
percussive welcome to join the shuffling.

One
and two *and,* one,
and two, *and* one...

quarter notes punctuating
each inch of sun that lowers
itself into the ocean (nature
as a single mother in the tub,
pinot and lavender

incense after a long day
of being taken for granted)

the smell of strong refer,
the burnouts that invite us in,
call us a *Hollywood couple*.
I have knocked out men
for less than this but one look
and you'd have known
how genuine their sentiment,

that there were moments
preceding this one, moments
of Bogart and Mary Astor
that flooded the funnel
of their experience and drained
to that point, to those words.

His words, his face, your face,
your words, and other words
that roll through my mind,
an epigraph to this place in time:
the voice of your eyes is deeper
than all roses, nobody
not even the rain has such small hands.

This moment's past light cone,
and all the agents that ride along
and each piece of them,
down to their sub atomic bones,
have contexts and carry them like anchors.

Pasts overlap in a limitless bouquet.
It is really quite precise, though,
the sum of it all what a man sees

when his life flashes before his eyes;
the breadth of it all,
what God sees,
always.

Symmetry

i.

This body expends itself, the sack
of my skin wets and dries at points
where cities and days it rains intersect.

This happens again and again,
then the snow melts and the flakes
of me are no longer discernible
from the dried leaves of autumn
or the road sand left from the nearest winter.

ii.

The last of my energy transfers.
All of it is here in the ether,
the beautiful ideals and the façade,
my attempt to replicate the ideals.
Only a gambling man, without illusions
of the house fix or the utter randomness
of how things come to be, could wager
on his next blip within the multiverse.

iii.

It is like the last place in every sense,
but not the last place, and I have a son.
I teach him how to watch the ball
hit the bat, and the value of top swing.
He does not listen, dips his shoulder,
whiffs and spins like a top each time

he gets an inside pitch.

iv.

We go to church every Sunday,
not for the creeds, but for the deep
oak finish of the pews and to see a sun,
just like the other one, but different,
shine strong through stained glass;
a small win for man taming pure light
for the picture he needs.

One day he asks me if I believe in God,
and I ask him why our world is a sphere.
We argue over who should answer first.
I tell him yes, and he shows me how
his paper plate becomes the same half circle
no matter where he folds.

This is because there is only one side, he says, *or because
there are many sides, so many you can't see, like germs.*
He stops, thinks for a moment, and speaks again.
I'm not sure there is much difference between the two.

The Death of Star

The star girl looked like a normal girl,
but she was brimming,
her pretty figure sated
with the best stuff of the universe.

It would have taken more
than this lifetime
to identify all the parts of her.

The star girl went dark
before the world was ready,
and so I merely
saw her in her three dimensions,
couldn't be certain of her topography,
and could only theorize
about what made her shine
but still...

Infinity is a melancholy science,
innumerable voices speaking,
a choir that goes unheard.
This is why man dies
and lives in painful disbelief:
so God can make sense
of the prayers of the devout.

My prayer, that what moves
in her now, wherever she is,
speeds, and heats, and fuses,
and expands, so that her grace

may roll out across the void,
a brave new world for us to cling to.

About the Author

Christopher Grillo is the author of Heroes' Tunnel (Anaphora Literary Press, 2015). His poems appear in Drunk Monkeys, Sport Literate, Biline, Spry, Aethlon, and more. Grillo is a graduate of the University of New Haven where he played strong safety for the Chargers, and of Southern Connecticut State University's MFA program. He lives and works in New Haven, Connecticut as an 8th grade language arts teacher and moonlights as an assistant football coach at his high school alma mater.

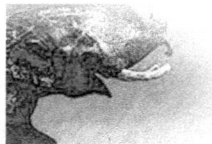